Applewood Books
Carlisle, Massachusetts

978-1-4290-9414-6

To inquire about this edition
or to request a free copy
of our current catalog
featuring our best-selling books, write to:
Applewood Books
P.O. Box 27
Carlisle, MA 01741
For more complete listings,
visit us on the web at:
www.awb.com

10 9 8 7 6 5 4 3 2 1
MANUFACTURED IN THE UNITED STATES OF AMERICA

Water: it is one of the most evocative of the elements. Without it all life would perish, but when it's uncontrolled, humans and landscapes are no match for its power. As you will see in this volume of quotations, water has been one of the most powerful symbols throughout the ages. Depths of water have always symbolized the soul and unknowable mysteries. And its rejuvenating properties make it the symbol for the fulfillment of every type of thirst.

Water's gentle persistence has been the inspiration of mystics, poets, and sages for as long as humans have been on this earth. German novelist Hermann Hesse captures this sentiment beautifully in *Siddhartha,* when he writes that "gentleness is stronger than severity, water is stronger than rock, love is stronger than force." And American poet Wallace Stevens says, "Human nature is like

III

water. It takes the shape of its container." The seeming paradox that water is able to take the shape of its container without resistance, while also being able to carve shapes into the hardest surfaces, has provided profound inspiration for generations of thinkers. This volume contains inspirational quotations from some of the most influential poets and scientists, spiritual leaders and philosophers, writers and thinkers of our time.

—Applewood Books

"Water is the driving force in nature."
—Leonardo da Vinci

"A lake is the landscape's most beautiful and expressive feature. It is the earth's eye; looking into which the beholder measures the depth of his own nature."
—Henry David Thoreau

"Rivers are roads which move, and which carry us whither we desire to go."
—Blaise Pascal

"We never know the worth of water till the well is dry."
—Thomas Fuller

"If these men do not take active conservation measures soon, I shall be forced to enter politics to plead for the conservation of the forests, wildflowers, the birds, and over and above everything else, the precious water on which our comfort, fertility, and life itself depend."

—Gene Stratton-Porter

"The water is the same on both sides of the boat."

—Finnish proverb

"I am not afraid of storms, for I'm learning to sail my ship."

—Louisa May Alcott

"High and fine literature is wine, and mine is only water; but everybody likes water."

—Mark Twain

"We ourselves feel that what we are doing is just a drop in the ocean. But the ocean would be less because of that missing drop."

—Mother Teresa

"Perhaps swimming was dancing under the water, he thought. To swim under lily pads seeing their green slender stalks wavering as you passed, to swim under upraised logs past schools of sunfish and bluegills, to swim through reed beds past wriggling water snakes and miniature turtles, to swim in small lakes, big lakes, Lake Michigan, to swim in small farm ponds, creeks, rivers, giant rivers where one was swept along easefully by the current, to swim naked alone at night when you were nineteen and so alone you felt like you were choking every waking moment, having left home for reasons more hormonal than rational."

—Jim Harrison

"Rest is not idleness, and to lie sometimes on the grass under trees on a summer's day, listening to the murmur of the water, or watching the clouds float across the sky, is by no means a waste of time."

—John Lubbock

"The sea is as near as we come to another world."

—Anne Stevenson

"I wanted freedom, open air and adventure. I found it on the sea."

—Alain Gerbault

"The man who is swimming against the stream knows the strength of it."

—Woodrow Wilson

"Civilization did not come with fire. It came with the discovery of how to use fire to heat water."

—Laura Anne Gilman

"It has always been a happy thought to me that the creek runs on all night, new every minute, whether I wish it or know it or care, as a closed book on a shelf continues to whisper to itself its own inexhaustible tale. So many things have been shown so to me on these banks, so much light has illumined me by reflection here where the water comes down, that I can hardly believe that this grace never flags, that the pouring from ever renewable sources is endless, impartial, and free."

—Annie Dillard

"We must go and see for ourselves."
  —Jacques Cousteau

"I have seen the sea when it is stormy and wild; when it is quiet and serene; when it is dark and moody. And in all its moods, I see myself."
  —Martin D. Buxbaum

"If I offer you a glass of water, and bring back a cup of ice, I'm trying to teach you patience. And also that sometimes you get ice with no water, and later you'll get water with no ice. Ah, but that's life, no?"
  —Jarod Kintz

"Water is nothing if not ingemination, an encore to the tenacity of life."
  —Terry Tempest Williams

"Therefore, just as water retains no constant shape, so in warfare there are no constant conditions."
  —Sun Tzu

"You can't trust water: Even a straight stick turns
crooked in it."

—W. C. Fields

"If you're a sailor, best not know how to swim.
Swimming only prolongs the inevitable—if the
sea wants you and your time has come."

—James Clavell

"[We are not satisfied and will not be satisfied]
until justice rolls down like water and
righteousness like a mighty stream."

—Martin Luther King Jr.

"Eventually, all things merge into one, and a
river runs through it. The river was cut by the
world's great flood and runs over rocks from
the basement of time. On some of the rocks
are timeless raindrops. Under the rocks are the
words, and some of the words are theirs. I am
haunted by waters."

—Norman Maclean

"I really don't know why it is that all of us are so committed to the sea, except I think it's because in addition to the fact that the sea changes, and the light changes, and ships change, it's because we all came from the sea. And it is an interesting biological fact that all of us have in our veins the exact same percentage of salt in our blood that exists in the ocean, and, therefore, we have salt in our blood, in our sweat, in our tears. We are tied to the ocean. And when we go back to the sea—whether it is to sail or to watch it—we are going back from whence we came."

—John F. Kennedy

"Ocean, n. A body of water occupying about two-thirds of a world made for man—who has no gills."

—Ambrose Bierce

"In one drop of water are found all the secrets of all the oceans; in one aspect of You are found all the aspects of existence."

—Khalil Gibran

"'For the people of my country,' Renato said,
    'water is everything: love, life, religion…even
    God.'
'It is like that for me too,' I said. 'In English we
    call that a metaphor.'
'Of course,' said Renato, 'and water is the most
    abundant metaphor on the earth.'"
    —Pam Houston

"The sea does not reward those who are too
anxious, too greedy, or too impatient. One should
lie empty, open, choiceless as a beach—waiting
for a gift from the sea."
    —Anne Morrow Lindbergh

"Water does not resist. Water flows. When you
plunge your hand into it, all you feel is a caress.
Water is not a solid wall, it will not stop you.
But water always goes where it wants to go, and
nothing in the end can stand against it. Water
is patient. Dripping water wears away a stone.
Remember that, my child. Remember you are
half water. If you can't go through an obstacle, go
around it. Water does."
    —Margaret Atwood

"The sea has never been friendly to man. At most it has been the accomplice of human restlessness."

—Joseph Conrad

"If gold has been prized because it is the most inert element, changeless and incorruptible, water is prized for the opposite reason—its fluidity, mobility, changeability that make it a necessity and a metaphor for life itself. To value gold over water is to value economy over ecology, that which can be locked up over that which reconnects all things."

—Rebecca Solnit

"If one morning I walked on top of the water across the Potomac River, the headline that afternoon would read: 'President Can't Swim.'"

—Lyndon B. Johnson

"It is rooted deep in your bones; the water calls out to you until it causes you physical pain unless you come to it."

—Nadia Scrieva

"She was free in her wildness. She was a wanderess, a drop of free water. She belonged to no man and to no city."

—Roman Payne

"A lake carries you into recesses of feeling otherwise impenetrable."

—William Wordsworth

"I find myself at the extremity of a long beach. How gladly does the spirit leap forth, and suddenly enlarge its sense of being to the full extent of the broad, blue, sunny deep! A greeting and a homage to the Sea! I descend over its margin, and dip my hand into the wave that meets me, and bathe my brow. That far-resounding roar is the Ocean's voice of welcome. His salt breath brings a blessing along with it."

—Nathaniel Hawthorne

"Water belongs to us all. Nature did not make the sun one person's property, nor air, nor water, cool and clear."

—Ovid

"The lakes are something you are unprepared
for...the forest is diminished to a fine fringe on
their edges, with here and there a blue mountain,
like amethyst jewels set around some jewel of
the first water—so anterior, so superior, to all the
changes that are to take place on their shores,
even now civil and refined, and fair as they can
ever be."
  —Henry David Thoreau

"The great question of the seventies is, shall
we surrender to our surroundings, or shall we
make our peace with nature and begin to make
reparations for the damage we have done to our
air, to our land, and to our water?"
  —Richard Nixon

"Dip him in the river who loves water."
  —William Blake

"We are on the Colorado...that means something
more to me than thoughts of electrical power or a
harnessed river."
  —Barry Goldwater

"For whatever we lose (like a you or a me),
It's always ourself we find in the sea."

—E. E. Cummings

"It is life, I think, to watch the water. A man can learn so many things."

—Nicholas Sparks

"Running water never grows stale, so you just have to keep on flowing."

—Bruce Lee

"If snow melts down to water, does it still remember being snow?"

—Jennifer McMahon

"…The river sliding along its banks, darker now
    than the sky
descending a last time to scatter its diamonds
    into these black
waters that contain the day that passed, the night
    to come."

—Philip Levine

"All good writing is swimming under water and
holding your breath."

—F. Scott Fitzgerald

"Let the rain kiss you."

—Langston Hughes

"The water you kids were playing in, he said,
had probably been to Africa and the North Pole.
Genghis Khan or Saint Peter or even Jesus may
have drunk it. Cleopatra might have bathed in it.
Crazy Horse might have watered his pony with
it. Sometimes water was liquid. Sometimes it was
rock hard—ice. Sometimes it was soft—snow.
Sometimes it was visible but weightless—clouds.
And sometimes it was completely invisible—
vapor—floating up into the sky like the souls of
dead people. There was nothing like water in the
world, Jim said. It made the desert bloom but
also turned rich bottomland into swamp. Without
it we'd die, but it could also kill us, and that was
why we loved it, even craved it, but also feared
it. Never take water for granted, Jim said. Always
cherish it. Always beware of it."

—Jeannette Walls

"Filthy water cannot be washed."

—African proverb

"The sea pronounces something, over and over,
in a hoarse whisper; I cannot quite make it out."

—Annie Dillard

"Hark, now hear the sailors cry
Smell the sea, and feel the sky
Let your soul and spirit fly
Into the mystic."

—Van Morrison

"Did you ever feel the tongue dry, the lips
parched, and the throat feverish, and then,
bringing a goblet filled with pure water to your
lips, do you remember the sensation as it trickled
over your tongue and gurgled down your throat?
Was it not a luxury?"

—John Bartholomew Gough

"Every time we walk along a beach some ancient
urge disturbs us so that we find ourselves
shedding shoes and garments, or scavenging
among seaweed and whitened timbers like the
homesick refugees of a long war."

—Loren C. Eiseley

"Ah, well, then you've never stood on a beach as
the waves came crashing in, the water stretching
out from you until it's beyond sight, moving and
blue and alive and so much bigger than even
the black beyond seems because the ocean hides
what it contains."

—Patrick Ness

"The great sea makes one a great sceptic."

—Richard Jefferies

"The tides are in our veins."

—Robinson Jeffers

"Rain is grace; rain is the sky descending to the earth; without rain, there would be no life."

—John Updike

"A person should go out on the water on a fine day to a small distance from a beautiful coast, if he would see Nature really smile. Never does she look so delightful, as when the sun is brightly reflected by the water, while the waves are gently rippling, and the prospect receives life and animation from the glancing transit of an occasional row-boat, and the quieter motion of a few small vessels. But the land must be well in sight; not only for its own sake, but because the immensity and awfulness of a mere sea-view would ill accord with the other parts of the glittering and joyous scene."

—Augustus William Hare and Julius Charles Hare

"It is a curious situation that the sea, from which life first arose should now be threatened by the activities of one form of that life. But the sea, though changed in a sinister way, will continue to exist; the threat is rather to life itself."

—Rachel Carson

"If there is magic on this planet, it is contained in water."

—Loren C. Eiseley

"We are all bodies of water, guarding the mystery of our depths…"

—Deborah Smith

"Be wary of the man who does not offer water, charges too much for water, asks for too much water, and the one who makes water his business."

—Suzy Kassem

"Long before we saw the sea, its spray was on our lips, and showered salt rain upon us."

—Charles Dickens

"Relationships are like water. If you grab tight, clamping and clenching to gain control, you'll lose it all. Instead, cup your hand gently, so she feels free to drink until her thirst is quenched."

—Jarod Kintz

"I believe that water is the only drink for a wise man."

—Henry David Thoreau

"When you're young, there's so much that you can't take in. It's pouring over you like a waterfall. When you're older, it's less intense, but you're able to reach out and drink it. I love being older."

—Sigourney Weaver

"Water is sufficient…the spirit moves over water."

—Friedrich Nietzsche

"Have you also learned that secret from the river; that there is no such thing as time? That the river is everywhere at the same time, at the source and at the mouth, at the waterfall, at the ferry, at the current, in the ocean and in the mountains, everywhere and that the present only exists for it, not the shadow of the past nor the shadow of the future."

—Hermann Hesse

"If the private life of the sea could ever be
transposed onto paper, it would talk not about
rivers or rain or glaciers or of molecules of
oxygen and hydrogen, but of the millions of
encounters its waters have shared with creatures
of another nature."

—Federico Chini

"The cure for anything is salt water—sweat,
tears, or the sea."

—Isak Dinesen

"Watch waterfalls of pity roar, you feel to moan
but unlike before, you discover that you'd just be
one more person crying."

—Bob Dylan

"A Breeze came wandering from the sky,
Light as the whispers of a dream;
He put the o'erhanging grasses by,
And softly stooped to kiss the stream,
The pretty stream, the flattered stream,
The shy, yet unreluctant stream."

—William Cullen Bryant

"In a swamp, as in meditation, you begin
to glimpse how elusive, how inherently
insubstantial, how fleeting our thoughts are, our
identities. There is magic in this moist world,
in how the mind lets go, slips into sleepy water,
circles and nuzzles the banks of palmetto and
wild iris, how it seeps across dreams, smears
them into the upright world, rots the wood of
treasure chests, welcomes the body home."
　　—Barbara Hurd

"Secrets press inside a person. They press the
way water presses at a dam. The secrets and the
water, they both want to get out."
　　—Franny Billingsley

"Too much of water hast thou, poor Ophelia,
And therefore I forbid my tears."
　　—William Shakespeare

"Don't be ashamed to weep; 'tis right to grieve.
Tears are only water, and flowers, trees, and fruit
cannot grow without water."
　　—Brian Jacques

"Let the most absent-minded of men be plunged in his deepest reveries—stand that man on his legs, set his feet a-going, and he will infallibly lead you to water, if water there be in all that region. Should you ever be athirst in the great American desert, try this experiment, if your caravan happens to be supplied with a metaphysical professor. Yes, as everyone knows, meditation and water are wedded forever."

—Herman Melville

"Pure water is the world's first and foremost medicine."

—Slovakian proverb

"Romance often begins by a splashing waterfall and ends over a leaky sink."

—Ellen DeGeneres

"Love flows like flowers, and grows like water. I'm so thirsty for romance I could drink a dozen roses."

—Jarod Kintz

"What makes the desert beautiful is that
somewhere it hides a well."
—Antoine de Saint-Exupéry

"Plans to protect air and water, wilderness and
wildlife are in fact plans to protect man."
—Stewart Udall

"Land and water are not really separate things,
but they are separate words, and we perceive
through words."
—David Rains Wallace

"There brews He beautiful water! And beautiful
it always is! You see it glistening in the dewdrop;
you hear it singing in the summer rain; you
see it sparkling in the ice gem when the trees
seem loaded with rich jewels!…dancing in the
hailstorm, leaping, foaming, dashing…! See how
it weaves a golden gauze for the setting sun, and
a silvery tissue for the midnight moon!"
—John Bartholomew Gough

"They both listened silently to the water, which to them was not just water, but the voice of life, the voice of Being, the voice of perpetual Becoming."

—Hermann Hesse

"In the desert, the only god is a well."

—Vera Nazarian

"Down through the valley and over the hill,
    Where the bluebird calls to the whippoorwill;
    Where the buttercups and the daisies grow,
    And the Summer breezes, so gently, blow,
There is a tiny brook that wends its way
    As it twists and it turns, where'er it may;
    And over each glistening stone it brings
    To us the rippling song that it sings."

—Gertrude Tooley Buckingham

"My mind is a raging torrent, flooded with rivulets of thought cascading into a waterfall of creative alternatives."

—Mel Brooks

"I spin on the circle of wave upon wave of the
sea."

—Pablo Neruda

"Water seeks its own level. Look at them. The
Tigris, the Euphrates, the Mississippi, the
Amazon, the Yangtze. The world's greatest
rivers. And every one of them finds its way to the
ocean."

—Alison McGhee

"And I feel like the Queen of Water. I feel like
water that transforms from a flowing river
to a tranquil lake to a powerful waterfall to a
freshwater spring to a meandering creek to a
salty sea to raindrops gentle on your face to hard,
stinging hail to frost on a mountaintop, and back
to a river again."

—Laura Resau

"How inappropriate to call this planet Earth
when it is clearly Ocean."

—Arthur C. Clarke

"Just keep swimming. Just keep swimming. Just keep swimming, swimming, swimming."

—Dory from *Finding Nemo*

"Homeopaths argue that water has a memory."

—Scarlett Thomas

"An over-indulgence of anything, even something as pure as water, can intoxicate."

—Criss Jami

"Do not turn me into restless waters if you cannot promise to be my stream."

—Sanober Khan

"As long as I live, I'll hear waterfalls and birds and winds sing. I'll interpret the rocks, learn the language of flood, storm, and the avalanche. I'll acquaint myself with the glaciers and wild gardens, and get as near the heart of the world as I can."

—John Muir

"Life in us is like the water in a river."

—Henry David Thoreau

"She dares me to pour myself out like a living waterfall. She dares me to enter the soul that is more than my own; she extinguishes fear in mere seconds. She lets light come through."

—Virginia Woolf

"I love you like a river that understands that it must learn to flow differently over waterfalls and to rest in the shallows. I love you because we are all born in the same place, at the same source, which keeps us provided with a constant supply of water. And so, when we feel weak, all we have to do is wait a little. The spring returns, and the winter snows melt and fill us with new energy."

—Paulo Coelho

"The places where water comes together with other water. Those places stand out in my mind like holy places."

—Raymond Carver

"We shall not cease from exploration
And the end of all our exploring
Will be to arrive where we started
And know the place for the first time.
Through the unknown, remembered gate
When the last of earth left to discover
Is that which was the beginning;
At the source of the longest river
The voice of the hidden waterfall
And the children in the apple-tree
Not known, because not looked for
But heard, half-heard, in the stillness
Between two waves of the sea."

   —T. S. Eliot

"You are water
I'm water
we're all water in different containers
that's why it's so easy to meet
someday we'll evaporate together."

   —Yoko Ono

"Gentleness is stronger than severity, water is
stronger than rock, love is stronger than force."

   —Hermann Hesse

"Because of the Thames I have always loved inland waterways—water in general, water sounds—there's music in water. Brooks babbling, fountains splashing. Weirs, waterfalls; tumbling, gushing."

—Julie Andrews

"All water is holy water."

—Rajiv Joseph

"I'm surfing the giant life wave."

—William Shatner

"Good luck and Good work for the happy mountain raindrops, each one of them a high waterfall in itself, descending from the cliffs and hollows of the clouds to the cliffs and hollows of the rocks, out of the sky-thunder into the thunder of the falling rivers."

—John Muir